CORYTHOSAURUS

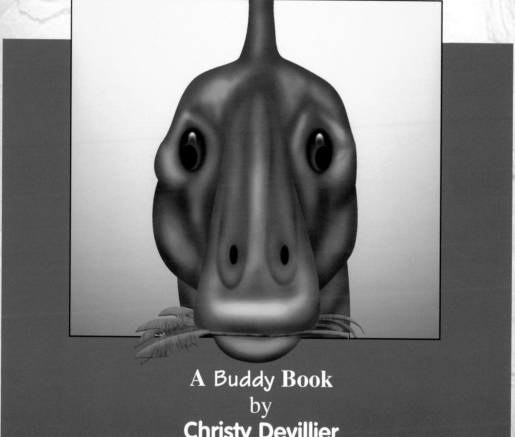

A Buddy Book
by
Christy Devillier

ABDO
Publishing Company

Published by ABDO Publishing Company, 4940 Viking Drive, Edina, Minnesota 55435. Copyright © 2004 by Abdo Consulting Group, Inc. International copyrights reserved in all countries. No part of this book may be reproduced in any form without written permission from the publisher.

Printed in the United States.

Edited by: Michael P. Goecke
Contributing Editor: Matt Ray
Graphic Design: Denise Esner, Maria Hosley
Image Research: Deborah Coldiron
Illustrations: Deborah Coldiron
Photographs: Corel, Hulton Archives, Photodisc

Library of Congress Cataloging-in-Publication Data

Devillier, Christy, 1971-
    Corythosaurus/Christy Devillier.
       p. cm.
    Includes index.
    Summary: Describes the physical characteristics, habitat, and behavior of a crested, duck-billed dinosaur that lived about seventy million years ago.
    ISBN 1-59197-537-9
    1. Corythosaurus—Juvenile literature. [1. Corythosaurus. 2. Dinosaurs.] I. Title.

QE862.O65D48 2004
567.914—dc22

                                      2003057813

TABLE OF CONTENTS

The Corythosaurus was a duck-billed dinosaur. Duck-billed dinosaurs had hard beaks. The Corythosaurus also had a crest on its head. It lived about 70 million years ago.

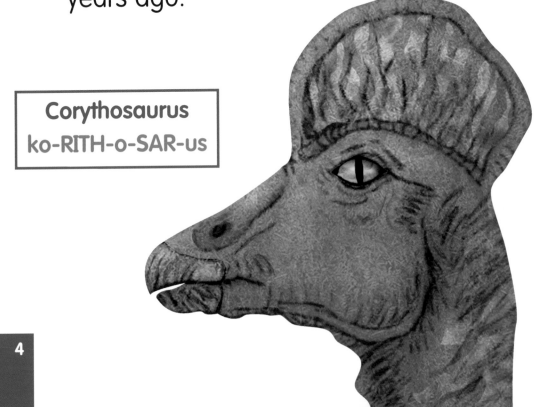

Corythosaurus
ko-RITH-o-SAR-us

4

The Corythosaurus was about
30 feet (nine m) long. It may have
weighed about 10,000 pounds
(4,500 kg). That is as heavy as
an elephant.

The Corythosaurus was about
as heavy as an elephant.

HOW DID THEY MOVE?

Scientists believe the Corythosaurus could move fast. They believe it ran or walked on its two back legs. The Corythosaurus probably walked on all four legs, too. Its back legs were longer than its front legs.

TAIL

The Corythosaurus had a long, heavy tail. The sides of the tail were mostly flat. This kind of tail would help the Corythosaurus swim. Many scientists believe this dinosaur was a good swimmer.

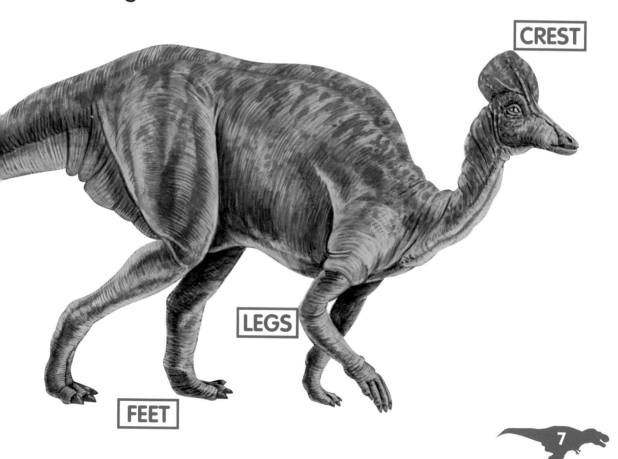

CREST

LEGS

FEET

WHY WERE THEY SPECIAL?

Corythosaurus means "helmet lizard." Scientists named this dinosaur after its "helmet," or crest. The male Corythosaurus had a bigger crest than the female.

The Corythosaurus's crest was bony and hollow. It had many tubes. These tubes went from the dinosaur's nose to its throat.

The Corythosaurus had a crest on its head.

Scientists have many ideas about the Corythosaurus's crest. Maybe the Corythosaurus used its crest to make honking sounds. Maybe the crest gave the Corythosaurus a better sense of smell. It could have used its crest to cool itself, too.

WHERE DID THEY LIVE?

The Corythosaurus lived in North America. It lived on land that is now Montana and Alberta, Canada.

The Corythosaurus lived during the late Cretaceous period. Back then, the world was different. The weather was tropical. Forests covered the land. The forests were full of evergreens, palms, and flowering plants.

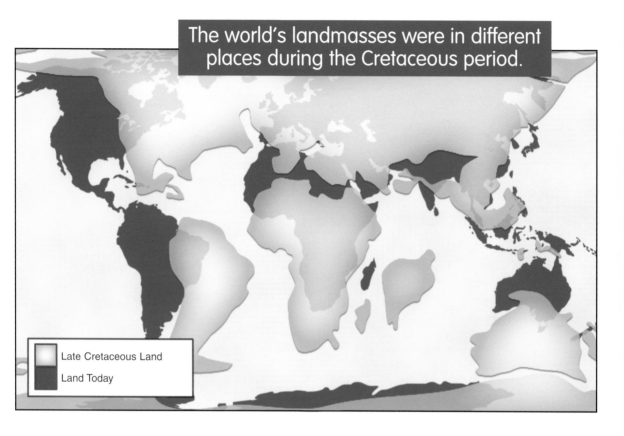

The world's landmasses were in different places during the Cretaceous period.

Late Cretaceous Land

Land Today

Scientists believe the Corythosaurus lived in wet areas. It probably lived near swamps.

WHAT DID THEY EAT?

The Corythosaurus was an herbivore. Herbivores eat plants. The Corythosaurus may have eaten leaves, pine needles, fruits, and seeds. It may have eaten from magnolias, ginkgoes, palms, and evergreen trees.

The Corythosaurus ate with a hard beak.

The Corythosaurus ate plants with its beak. This beak had no teeth. But the Corythosaurus had hundreds of teeth in its cheeks. It chewed food with these teeth.

WHO WERE THEIR ENEMIES?

Many meat-eating dinosaurs lived during the Corythosaurus's time. One of them was the Albertosaurus. It may have hunted the Corythosaurus's young.

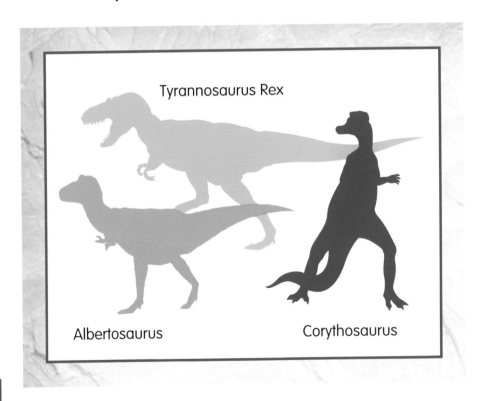

Tyrannosaurus Rex

Albertosaurus

Corythosaurus

The Albertosaurus was related to the Tyrannosaurus rex. Both dinosaurs had sharp teeth and a strong mouth for biting. Scientists believe the Albertosaurus could run fast on its two strong legs. Its speed would help it catch prey.

Scientists believe the Corythosaurus did not fight predators. They think it ran away when danger was near. Having keen eyesight and hearing would help it spot danger quickly.

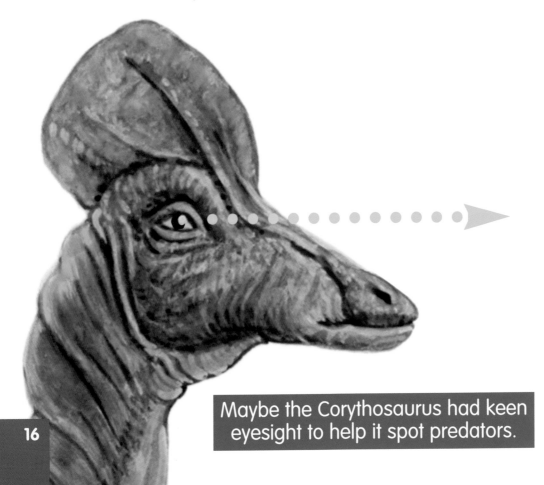

Maybe the Corythosaurus had keen eyesight to help it spot predators.

Scientists believe the Corythosaurus lived in groups called herds. This would help it stay safe from predators. Herd members could warn each other when danger was near. Maybe the Corythosaurus gave warning calls with its crest.

17

Dinosaurs laid eggs. Scientists believe the Corythosaurus left the swamp to lay their eggs. It built nests of mud on higher ground. The Corythosaurus mothers may have watched over the nest. They may have fed and protected their young.

Dinosaur egg fossils

THE FAMILY TREE

The Corythosaurus belonged to the Hadrosauridae family. Hadrosaurs lived in many places around the world. Their fossils have been found in North America, Europe, and Asia.

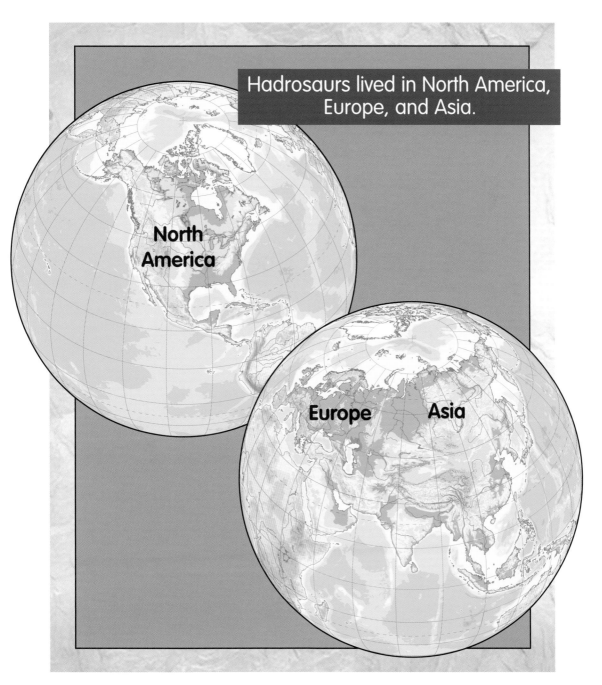

Hadrosaurs lived in North America, Europe, and Asia.

North America

Europe   Asia

Hadrosaurs were duck-billed dinosaurs. They ate plants with a toothless beak. Some hadrosaurs had special pouches in their mouth for storing food.

Not all of the hadrosaurs had a crest. One of these crestless hadrosaurs was the Edmontosaurus.

The Edmontosaurus did not have a crest.

The Edmontosaurus lived in western North America about 70 million years ago. It was about 40 feet (12 m) long. This hadrosaur had bumps along its neck, back, and tail.

23

DISCOVERY

All the dinosaurs died out about 65 million years ago. This happened millions of years before people walked the earth.

People know about dinosaurs from studying their fossils. A fossil can be a bone or a footprint. Any trace of life from long ago is a fossil.

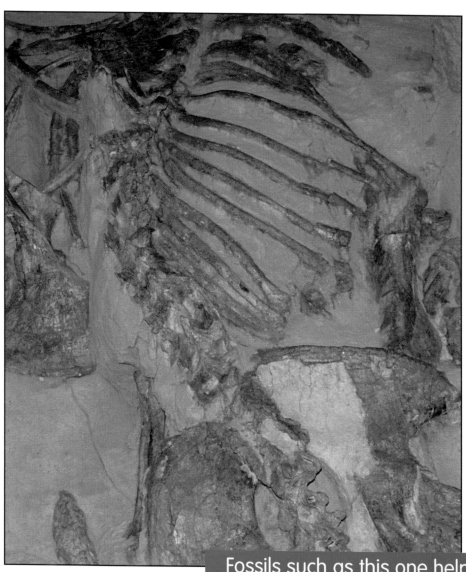

Fossils such as this one help people learn about dinosaurs.

Scientists called paleontologists study dinosaur fossils. Barnum Brown was a famous paleontologist. He discovered many dinosaurs.

Brown found the first Corythosaurus fossils in Alberta, Canada. He named the Corythosaurus in 1914.

Barnum Brown digging for dinosaur fossils in 1940.

WHERE ARE THEY TODAY?

American Museum of Natural History
Central Park West at 79th Street
New York, NY 10024-5192
www.amnh.org

Smithsonian National Museum of Natural History
10th Street and Constitution Avenue NW
Washington, D.C. 20560
www.nmnh.si.edu/paleo/dino/corynew.htm

Peabody Museum of Natural History
Yale University
170 Whitney Avenue
New Haven, CT 06520-8118
www.peabody.yale.edu

CORYTHOSAURUS

NAME MEANS	Helmet lizard
DIET	Plants
WEIGHT	10,000 pounds (4,500 kg)
LENGTH	30 feet (9 m)
TIME	Late Cretaceous period
ANOTHER HADROSAUR	Edmontosaurus
SPECIAL FEATURE	Crest
FOSSILS FOUND	USA—Montana Canada—Alberta

The Corythosaurus lived
70 million years ago.

The first humans appeared
1.6 million years ago.

Triassic Period	Jurassic Period	Cretaceous Period	Tertiary Period
245 Million years ago	208 Million years ago	144 Million years ago	65 Million years ago

Mesozoic Era

Cenozoic Era

WEB SITES

To learn more about the Corythosaurus, visit ABDO Publishing Company on the World Wide Web. Web sites about the Corythosaurus are featured on our "Book Links" page. These links are routinely monitored and updated to provide the most current information available.

www.abdopub.com

IMPORTANT WORDS

Cretaceous period a period of time that happened 144–65 million years ago.

dinosaur a reptile that lived on land 248–65 million years ago.

fossil remains of very old animals and plants commonly found in the ground. A fossil can be a bone, a footprint, or any trace of life.

herbivore a plant-eater.

hollow describes something that is empty on the inside.

paleontologist someone who studies very old life, such as dinosaurs, mostly by studying fossils.

predator an animal that hunts and eats other animals.

prey an animal that is food for other animals.

tropical weather that is warm and wet.

31

INDEX